From Surviving to Sustaining

Timeless Lessons from History's Greatest Survivors

Dr. Tanwin Mohammad Salauddin Ashrafi

Miss. Arfa Mohammad Salauddin Ashrafi

Copyright Page

ISBN: **978-93-5717-686-6**

Published independently through Amazon Kindle Direct Publishing (KDP).

Publisher: Self-published by the authors.

First Edition – 2026

Disclaimer

From Surviving to Sustaining is written solely for the educational and information purposes. The interpretation and analysis of this book are based on historical records, publicly available information, and the authors' perspectives. While writing efforts are taken to make sure of the accuracy and reliability of the information of the contents, authors make no representations or warranties regarding the completeness, applicability to individual circumstances. Readers are encouraged to use their own intellectual to make their own judgements. The mention historical events, figures, organizations or institutions are used only for educational purposes. Such references do not mean to get affiliation or approval by the individuals or organizations mentioned. The authors and publisher shall not be held responsible for any kind of damage, loss, and consequences arising from the use of the information contained in this book.

Preface

Today's contemporary era is characterized by rapid transformation, complex challenges from daily routine to global problems, these lead to increase the uncertainty in the human behavior and outcomes. In such an environment, survival is not the alone target to achieve, rather, sustainable progress is demands. Adaptability, strategic foresight, ethical grounding, and the capacity to transform crisis into constructive advancement are important abilities requires for sustainable progress. This book was born from a simple yet powerful question: Is surviving sufficient in an age that constantly tests our limits?

Literature reviews help to understand the concept of survival, it has been observed that humans always stood at the edge of uncertainty and chosen not merely to endure, but to evolve. Explorers braved the unknown, reformers challenged injustice, scientists reshaped understanding, and innovators redefined possibility. Their stories reveal that survival is only the first step. What truly shapes the future is the ability to sustain with the help of values, vision, learning, and collective strength.

In this study, we realized that the journey from surviving to sustaining is not reserved for extraordinary figures alone. It is a path available to each of us as individuals. Whether in personal challenges or in helping the global transformation, the principles remain the same: purpose-based resilience, trust-based cooperation, and responsibility-based innovation.

This book is divided into three main parts, to build the foundation of Survival, Sustaining, and Thriving. These parts are built on each other, tracing the development to survive towards the sustainability and then finally to visionary growth. The aim of tis book is not to gather information or historical achievements but to extract timeless lessons that can guide readers for their future endorsements.

This book is for those who seek more than temporary solutions. It is for those who think that strength is not in surviving but sustaining; purpose is not sustaining but to progress and future is in their hand to shape with intention. If this book encourages even one reader to move beyond mere survival toward meaningful, lasting growth, then its purpose will have been fulfilled.

Introduction

According to historical records, the main goal of humans in any era is survival. From the navigators, explorers, astronomers and cultures records, who battled to know the unknown, had redefined our understanding of life. Although, humanity has constantly tested the limits of endurance. But just surviving has never been enough. The real definition of progress is not just getting through difficult situations but turning them into strength. It is about learning how to survive, adapt, and ultimately perform effectively. This book, *From Surviving to Sustaining*, is a journey that shows how these transformations have happened. It demonstrates how people and even civilizations have turned instances of difficulties into opportunities to grow, come up with new ideas, and start over. Over the centuries, hunger, conflict, isolation, failure, or the uncertainty of the future were different forms of challenges. These challenges got responses that lead to triumph remain timeless: courage, adaptability, vision, and the power of human connection. By analyzing different historical events, this book offers readers both wisdom and practical insight into how we can navigate today's complex world with resilience and purpose.

Structure of the Book

From Surviving to Sustaining has three parts that are all connected. Each one builds on what was learnt in the ones before it, with the goal of long-term growth, endurance, and eventually visionary innovation.

Part I: Foundations of Survival is art which means adapting to changes, being strong and flexible. The first chapter Art of Survival in this part is based on Sir Ernest Shackleton's famous trip to Antarctica. A story about how people came together and led each other through terrible times. The next two chapters, "Adapting to Change" and "Strength of Character and Values," talk about the moral and scientific ideas that make people strong. These chapters show how people fight against the odds to protect themselves and others. The case studies of these chapters such as Charles Darwin's theory of evolution and Malala Yousafzai and Mahatma Gandhi, have great pedagogical values .

Part II: Sustaining in the Long Run shifts focus from survival to sustainability. This means studies of how short term achievements are converted into long term goals. This section studies scarcity, cooperation, and reflection and helps turn challenges into lasting opportunity. With the help of stories, such as lives of Abraham Lincoln, Nelson Mandela, Princess Diana, and Winston. This section reveals how sustaining one's purpose requires both flexibility and vision. It emphasizes that failure is not the contrary to success, instead of being its most genuine instructor. This section moves from recurring theme from Edison's experiments to the global lessons learned through climate action.

Part III: Thriving & Advanced Methodologies take the journey from most risky venture to the modern frontier of human progression. The sections shift from study of the age of innovation, foresight, into intelligent risk-taking decisions. It also explores pioneers' work of Steve Jobs and Elen Musk, studies the reinvention of themselves and their industries through creativity and courage. The chapter also explores the journey of OpenAI using strategic vision to anticipate future needs in the age of artificial intelligence. The section is concluded with chapter, *From Surviving to Sustaining* in Daily Life, which translates learned lessons into practical routines to achieve personal and professional balance, while explaining how resilience and flexibility can influence our daily development.

Table of Content

Part I: Foundations of Survival

1

The Art of Survival

Introduction

Humans are one of the toughest animals in the world because of their spiritual power. When it is pushed to extreme level, it may reveal its truest character. One such event is seen in the story of Sir Ernest Shackleton. He was the most celebrated explorer of the Heroic Age of Antarctic Exploration. His journey in January 1915 is intended to land on Antarctic continent. The expedition did not achieve the first land crossing of the Antarctic continent. Instead, it became an unmatched example of how strong and brave humans can be when things seem impossible. This explorer was not just story to tell but also became an extraordinary study case to understand resilience, adaptability, and the raw art of survival.

Unlike the other explorers, whose works are remembered as conquests of the territories or scientific achievements, his journey exemplifies the ability to survive. It focuses more on human determination, improvisation, leadership, and the capacity to protect life against overwhelming odds. Their hardship long lasted for two whole years against nature with their ship, *Endurance*, trapped and eventually crushed in the Weddell Sea pack ice. Remarkably, despite the catastrophic setbacks, not a single man of Shackleton's 28-member crew perished. This journey emphasizes the need of preparation for unforeseen circumstances, leadership, and collaborative effort, as well as physical stamina and mental strength. His decisions, personality, and leadership style transformed what could have been a mass tragedy into one of history's greatest epics of survival, exemplify "The Art of Survival".

Survival by Leadership: Lessons from the Endurance Expedition

Shackleton's Vision and the Road to Antarctica

To understand Shackleton's story of survival, it is important to know what he wanted to achieve. He was born in 1874 in County Kildare, Ireland. In his early career, he worked as an officer in the merchant navy taught him how to be a good sailor and how to be tough, which are both important skills for travel. His first exploration of Antarctica was with Robert Falcon Scott's *Discovery* voyage in 1901. Later, in 1907, he led the Nimrod expedition, pushing closer to the South Pole than anyone before him. By 1914, other explorers not only had mapped Antarctica but also reached south pole. A notable success was achieved by Roald Amundsen through navigating the Northwest Passage and being the first to reach the South Pole in 1911. Other main obstacle was World War I of that era for any venture. Shackleton even provided the Admiralty with his crew and ship to help win the war. When told that the journey ought to move forward, Shackleton collected a mixed company of sailors, scientists, and adventurers, many of whom had never experienced freezing conditions. Little did they realize that their aim of reaching Antarctica would be surpassed by a far more pressing one: survival.

The Trapping of Endurance

Endurance sailed in August 1914 with these diverse crew members. After 4 months, the ship entered the icy Weddell Sea. As they reached near to their intended destination on the Antarctic continent in January, the ship became trapped in thick ice. At first, he hoped for a thaw, but as weeks passed, the crew realized they were drifting helplessly with the ice. Here the first lesson to survival is unfolded: adaptation with rigid plan. He did not fall into doubt or depression. Instead, he began a methodical review of their situation. The crew was told to stick to a schedule as a form of psychological warfare to combat the soul-crushing routine and anxiety of their new, immobile life. Sports were organized, scientific observations maintained, and the ship's daily routines were strictly followed. This seemingly insignificant dedication to order was, in reality, the first and most important step towards survival. By October 1915, moving icebergs had damaged the Endurance. Shackleton calmly instructed the crew to abandon the ship and recover everything they could. Watching their ship, their last connection to civilization, collapse into the sea might have crushed spirits, but Shackleton famously told his troops, "Ship and stores have gone—now we must get on with the job." It was the basis of survival: no looking back, just ahead.

Life on the Ice

The crew started the new section of the long journey to survive on the iceberg with limited food supply to survive and only three lifeboats. Here, he demonstrated the quality of good leadership by shared food equally, even relinquishing his own rations at times, discouraged pessimism and maintained optimism through rituals, jokes, and shared activities, encouraged keeping diaries and scientific observations, providing a sense of purpose beyond survival. The art of survival is not only about physical endurance but also the management of morale. Shackleton understood that despair kills as effectively as hunger or cold. By framing their plight as a collective challenge, he kept the men engaged. Although, this has not lasted for long. As the iceberg breaks, they have to abandon it. They start their journey toward the solid ground with the help of 3 lifeboats.

The Lifeboats to Elephant Island

Even though this was a journey of determination during that period, ultimately becoming one of the most remarkable survival achievements in history. These lifeboats, namely *James Caird*, *Stancomb Wills*, and *Dudley Docker*, moved through the freezing water and huge waves for seven days. Finally, the group reached the desert island, known as Elephant Island. It was both a success and a challenge to land on Elephant Island. The crew members were on safe ground, but help was still far away. There were no shipping routes nearby, so it was very unlikely that anyone would see them. Shackleton knew that something had to be done right away.

The James Caird *Voyage: Shackleton's Gamble*

He made bold decision and chose five members; especially those who can survive harsh conditions with one of the lifeboat *James Caird.* Others were instructed to remain in unity among each other. *The James Caird* voyage lasted 16 harrowing days. Navigated by Frank Worsley with remarkable precision, they battled hurricane-force winds and waves towering like buildings. At one point, the boat was nearly swamped by an iceberg-calved wave. They survived on meager rations of pemmican, biscuits, and melted ice. At last, the South Georgia Island greet them on May 10, 1916. Shackleton and two other men landed on the wrong side of the island and had to go through one last challenge: they had to cross the island's unmapped, rough interior without the right gear and get to the Stromness whaling station after 36 hours of nonstop walking.

Rescue of the Crew

As a leader, he wasted no time on his own problems at station rather he focused about how quickly he could return for his men on Elephant Island. His determination underscores another survival principle: responsibility for others is as vital as responsibility for oneself.

After three failed attempts due to ice and weather, Shackleton finally returned in August 1916 aboard the Chilean tug Yelcho. Against all odds, every man of the Endurance crew was alive. Shackleton's image as a leader who prioritized lives over fame was cemented.

Chapter Summary

Shackleton's story not merely teach us avoiding death but sustaining hope, unity, and dignity in the face of overwhelming adversity. The following principle points emerge from his story:

1. Adaptability Over Rigidity: He abandoned his dream of crossing Antarctica without hesitation when survival became the priority. Where other explorers never leave their main goal. This shows flexibility, which helps him to understand survival is more important than any other goal.
2. Leadership as Shared Hardship: His idea of leadership is not monitoring crew members from above rather than his involvement with them for daily chores became benchmark as leader. Activities such as sharing rations, labor, and risks among crew fostered trust and loyalty toward him. His story well reflects thought that survival in extreme conditions requires collective efforts.
3. Psychological Resilience: with the help of daily routine, maintaining good humorous environment among members, and shared goals was as vital as securing food and shelter. These

activities keeping their spirit high was perhaps his greatest survival skill.

4. Calculated Risk-Taking: The Journey through James Caird voyage was bold choice, but it was based on careful judgment and necessity. He balanced boldness with realism, showing that survival sometimes demands risk when the alternative is certain doom.
5. Ethical Responsibility: Unlike Scott or others of his era, Shackleton placed survival above personal glory. His primary aim became saving his men. This sense of responsibility elevated his leadership and remains a model for crisis management.

Despite being in one of the most dangerous places on Earth, his soldiers managed to stay alive for two years. This was not a matter of coincidence; rather, it was the result of good leadership, flexibility, and tireless determination. This story reminds us that survival is both a physical and psychological challenge. It requires not only the ability to endure hardship but also the vision to inspire others, the wisdom to adapt, and the courage to take risks when necessary.

Bibliography

1. Alexander, Caroline. *The Endurance: Shackleton's Legendary Antarctic Expedition*. Alfred A. Knopf, 1998.
2. Huntford, Roland. *Shackleton*. London: Hodder & Stoughton, 1985.
3. Lansing, Alfred. *Endurance: Shackleton's Incredible Voyage*. Basic Books, 1959.
4. Preston, Diana. *A First Rate Tragedy: Robert Falcon Scott and the Race to the South Pole*. Houghton Mifflin, 1997.
5. Shackleton, Ernest. *South: The Endurance Expedition*. William Heinemann, 1919.
6. Smith, Michael. *Shackleton: By Endurance We Conquer*. Oneworld Publications, 2014.
7. Worsley, Frank. *Shackleton's Boat Journey*. London: Penguin, 1933.

2

Adapting to Change

Introduction

All living things want to stay alive in their environment, and this depends on how well they can adapt. So, adaptability is what makes sustainability possible. Changing how you act or how you deal with what is going on around you is how you adapt. According to Darwin's Theory of Evolution, it is not the strongest but the most adaptable who survives. This shows that flexibility and adjustment are the keys to growth and success.

What is Change?

There are many factors affects once behaviours such the origin, beliefs, races and even colour of their skin. The challenge is not when you are in your natural habitats; but when circumstances, surroundings, or circumstances change, requiring adaptation or adjustment. This not only opens the new paths to developing different skills for survival but also refined old ones. The greatest story is still the Human existence in earth environments. In initial stage, humans faced harsh climates, scarce resources, and constant threats from predators in earth environment.

Thereafter, they start adapting by learning new skills using tools, controlling fire, forming groups, and changing their ways of living according to their surroundings. His adaptability became the foundation of human progress. Over time, it was not physical strength but intelligence, cooperation, and flexibility that enabled humans to survive and gradually dominate the environment. Among well known scientific theories, changes and adaptations in nature are best explained by the Theory of Evolution by Natural Selection.

Survival of the Fittest

Who is Charles Darwin?

An English scientist and biologist, Mr. Charles Darwin, is best known for developing the Theory of Evolution by Natural Selection. In 1859, he released his well-known book on the "Origin of Species", which transformed people's understanding of life on Earth. Darwin believed that all species evolve throughout time, with natural selection serving as the primary driver of change. This means that creatures with features that are more suited to their surroundings are more likely to live, reproduce, and transmit those qualities on to future generations. His hypothesis formed after examining plants and animals aboard the Her Majesty's Ship (HMS) Beagle. One of his most famous studies was focused on the finches of the Galápagos Islands. He found that birds of the same species had various beak forms based on the type of food available on each island. Similarly, the example of giraffes demonstrates how individuals with longer necks lived better by reaching higher leaves and passed this characteristic on to future generations. His ideas demonstrated that life is constantly changing and that adaptation, not strength, is the key to survival. His thesis not only revolutionized biology forever but it also helped people grasp the importance of adaptation in all aspects of life.

What did Darwin Achieve from His Theory?

Charles Darwin's Theory of Evolution by Natural Selection resulted in numerous significant achievements:

- Explanation of the diversity in life: showing how all living things are connected and how they all came from the same ancestors.
- Changed scientific thinking: His idea set up a solid foundation for biology and transformed the way scientists examined plants, animals, and people.

- Natural selection process: Survival is dependent on adaptation rather than strength, which became an important scientific idea.
- A new understanding of humanity - His insights helped people see that humans, like animals, are subject to the same rules of evolution.

Based on above, Darwin revolutionized science by demonstrating that life is constantly vehemently changing and that adaptability is the genuine path to survival. Even though, this theory explains a lot but was first rejected at proposal.

The reason his theory was rejected at first

When Darwin first proposed his Theory of Evolution by Natural Selection, it was widely dismissed. The main reason was that his theories opposed popular religious beliefs at the time. Most individuals believed that God created all living beings in their current form, as recounted in religious writings. Theory suggests that species evolve over time and that humans and animals have common origins stunned society. Another factor was a lack of scientific evidence. Genetics and DNA have not been identified at that time; therefore, people consider it difficult to accept that traits could be passed down from generation to generation. As a result, his theory was criticized by that time scholars, researchers, and religious leaders vehemently. However, as more data from fossils, genetics, and biology became available, his hypothesis gained acceptance and is today regarded as one of the most important foundations of modern science. Finally, the concept of flexibility and rigidity is more likely to be the concern of our interest.

Flexibility or rigidity

Even though rigidity may provide short-term stability. But it eventually collapses when faced with unexpected challenges. On the other hand, flexibility helps survival in changing circumstances. Science, nature, and history all support this. When storms hit, trees that bend stay alive, whereas trees that do not break. In the same way, people have achieved success not because they are strong, but because they can adapt, produce new ideas, and work together. Darwin's theory supports this by showing that species that adapt to their environment survive, while those that do not alter die out. Flexibility is what allows for growth in all areas of life, such as nature, society, and people.

Chapter Summary

- **Adapting to change** is important for survival, as shown by Darwin's ideas.
- **What Darwin achieved:** He explained the diversity of life, transformed biology, introduced natural selection, inspired future research, and showed that humans are part of evolution.
- **Later acceptance:** With the discovery of genetics, fossils, and DNA, his theory was proven right and is now one of the most important foundations of modern science.
- **Learning outcome:** Just like in nature, humans also need to adapt to changes—whether in technology, society, or environment—in order to succeed.

Bibliography

1. Credits: Britannica, and biology textbooks, Charles Darwin, *On the Origin of Species*

3

Strength of Character and Values

Introduction

Being social animals, we, humans face many challenges, whether personal struggles, social injustices, or catastrophic global events. In adverse situations, material wealth, physical strength, or clever strategies alone rarely sustain a person or a society. What truly helps with survival, determination, and significant advancement is strength in one's character, rooted in deep principles. Character is not a superficial quality nor a matter of reputation; it is the inner reality of who we are when stripped of external presences. In contrast, values serve as incredibly powerful guiding lights, directing choices and behaviours when circumstances become dark and confusing.

With these in mind, there are three interconnected themes: the inner compass for hard times, the lessons of survival through non-violence as drawn from history, and the power of integrity as the guiding principle that transforms values into living reality. These three together show why strong character is not only an individual characteristic but a cultural need in an era where societies are deeply tested by inequality, conflict, and uncertainty.

The Inner Compass for Hard Times

1. What is the Inner Compass?

The phrase “inner compass” is a metaphor for the moral and spiritual thinking of a person. This phrase is exemplified by the concept where a sailor depends upon a compass to navigate stormy seas when landmarks vanish from sight; individuals rely on their inner compass when external supports collapse. This compass is not a physical device but rather the ethical and emotional framework of the individual. It is made up of honesty, courage, justice, and compassion as values. A person guided by it does not fall prey to despair, corruption, or blind conformity. Instead, they achieve a sense of stability by heeding their conscience.

2. Why Hard Times Reveal True Character?

While there is no threat; it is much easier to appear honest or brave. Hardship, however, strips away illusions. History is filled with moments where values were challenged and true character revealed. In difficult circumstances, a person's actions speak louder than their words, demonstrating their strength of character, guided by inner compass. Wars revealed both cruelty and remarkable acts of kindness from ordinary individuals. Even in private life, a person facing illness, financial ruin, or betrayal often discovers whether their values are genuine principles or fragile conveniences. Ultimately, it is in times of trial that we discover what we are truly made of.

3. The Components of the Inner Compass

The individual characteristics that shape the inner compass includes:

- **Resilience:** The ability to endure pain, loss, or uncertainty without losing one's sense of self.
- **Hope:** A forward-looking orientation that prevents despair. It is not blind optimism but the belief that meaning can be found even in suffering.
- **Moral clarity:** The ability to distinguish right from wrong even when both choices carry risks.
- **Self-discipline:** The power to resist temptations of fear, anger, or selfishness.

These qualities guide a person through difficult situations, keeping them steady when external conditions are harsh.

Historical Cases

Several historical examples demonstrate how the inner compass guides both individual and collective movements through challenging times. The stories of Indian freedom struggle, which was led by Mahatma Gandhi, reflect the true characteristics of strong character. At the same time, the American civil rights movement with Martin Luther King Jr, Nelson Mandela's role in post-apartheid reconciliation, and Malala Yousafzai's advocacy for girls' education are powerful case studies of this principle in action. Each of these are demonstrating profound strength of character. Also, the importance of values in human characters to transform societies is deeply echoed in these types of studies. We will now explore some of these examples in more detail to understand their core ideas.

Mahatma Gandhi and the Indian Freedom Struggle

The story in Indian freedom was not started by the arrival of Mahatma Gandhi on the political scene in India in start of 19th century, but it was started by Binsu Manki from 1771 and 1857 revolt was frequently terms as **First War of Indian Independence**. However, these figures laid the ground work to build the characters in individuals to fight for their freedom. Thereafter, the Indian freedom struggle becomes one of the best examples where the components of the inner compass play a vital role not only in shaping individual character but also in guiding collective national efforts. Mahatma Gandhi led campaigns of civil disobedience against British colonial rule from 1917 until 1930. This protest faced a lot of tough resistance, which resulted in imprisonment, beatings, and economic hardship, yet protesters spirit remained unbroken. Mahatma Gandhi, himself faced different challenges and even was jailed multiple times, yet each imprisonment seemed to strengthen rather than weaken his resolve. This *resilience*, a refusal to surrender and a clinging to hope, became the backbone of Indian freedom movement.

Hope is the central idea of this struggle. Gandhi ji consistently reminded Indians that freedom was not a dream but an eventual certainty if they held firmly to non-violence. His vision of independent India, where every religion will be respected and could live in harmony gave millions a reason to endure hardship.

Mahatma Gandhi emphasized the importance of *moral clarity* through non-violence (ahinsa) and truth (satyagraha), claiming that freedom obtained without ethical methods would be empty. Subhas Chandra Bose, on the other hand, viewed armed resistance and force as morally justified in the face of colonial oppression, believing that the urgency of liberation took priority over a strict commitment to non-violence. Gandhi's ideology, in contrast, transformed the fight from a political revolt to a moral awakening by refusing to attack the British and instead standing out for justice with dignity. The Salt March of 1930's, for instance, was not only about salt; it was also about showing how wrong it is to tax the people's basic necessities.

Being nonviolent took a lot of *self-discipline.* It meant that protesters did not fight back when they were hit. It meant keeping your anger, fear and hate in check. His own *self-discipline* was very strong because he trained himself in strict practices. Self discipline cannot be won unless individuals learn to master their own impulses. The discipline of millions of Indians who followed his example allowed non-violence to become a credible and powerful tool.

Malala Yousafzai and the Fight for Girls' Education

The early 2000s was a crucial time seen by the word, when a powerful force, know as Taliban take over the Pakistan's Swat Valley, transforming a once-thriving cultural and educational hub into a region of fear and suppression.

Extremist perspectives were enforced on people, the most serious of which was the prohibition on female education. Further, the situation became unrealistic since schools were damaged, teachers were threatened, and families had to keep their girls at home. For a number of young girls, schools suddenly became places where they weren't allowed to be, and their futures were put on hold so that they could follow the rules. This campaign of fear was not just about education; it was also about getting rid of women's voices, power, and involvement in society. In this situation, survival meant either going along with what was happening or saying no. This choice put both physical safety and one's own character and beliefs at risk.

At a young age, Malala chose to resist. Motivated by her father, Ziauddin Yousafzai, a devoted educator, she started a campaign against the Taliban's restrictions. Her most notable early contribution was anonymous blogging for the BBC Urdu service in 2009. Using the false name "Gul Makai," she documented her everyday experiences of attending school amidst threats, the widespread terror within her community, and her need for education. This act of her shows self *discipline*, where she did not let fear make her abandon her studies, and she kept following a strict routine of learning despite danger. The work revealed the brutality of the Taliban and the resolute willpower of young girls who continued to carry their books as symbols of *hope*.

On October 9, 2012, Malala's open rebellion resulted in a horrific turning point. On her way home from school, she was attacked by a Taliban shooter who shot her in the head. This act of brutality aimed to permanently silence her and destroy the growing fire of resistance. Rather, it initiated a worldwide movement. Malala's survival of the attack went beyond mere human bravery; it demonstrated the *resilience* of an idea: that education cannot be destroyed by violence. Her recovery in Birmingham, United Kingdom, not only restored her health but gave her a global stage. The assassination attempt highlighted the fragility of girls' rights in regions affected by extremism, while also underscoring the unwavering bravery of individuals prepared to sacrifice all for justice. After the attack, it reveals a remarkable strength of character.

Malala's account after the attack shows extraordinary strength of character. While others might have withdrawn into quiet following such horror, she emerged with greater purpose. Courage, for Malala, was not only the lack of fear but the will to act in its presence. Her acts, even when they put her life in danger, were motivated by her *moral clarity* and her strong belief that girls should have the right to an education. Values such as bravery, equality, and compassion serve as the moral standards that directs sustainable transformation. Malala's story illustrates that global transformation originates not from extensive resources or authority, but from individuals whose values are strong enough to withstand fear, and whose vision is broad enough to include all of humanity.

Princess Mako and the Choice of Love over Royal Status

Though there are countless examples of how strength of character influences society, it also plays a crucial role in shaping personal choices. A striking example is that of Princess Mako of Japan. Her story serves as powerful contemporary illustration of how strength of character, guided by values, provides direction through hard times. Unlike Gandhi, King, or Malala, whose struggles were on grand political scales, Princess Mako's decision was deeply personal, yet it highlighted the same universal components of the inner compass.

From 2017, Princess Mako faced relentless criticism from citizens of Japan and the media because of her marriage till 2021. She showed *resilience* by standing firm against cultural expectations and the monarchy's demands that she sacrifices personal happiness for public approval. Selection of own choice over her current status meant leaving behind privileges and financial security that escorted her role as a royal. Despite insecurity, she embraced it with *hope*, understanding that happiness could only come from following her heart. This hope was a valiant act, by placing faith in personal happiness and authenticity rather than external validation. She made her choice based on *moral clarity*, knowing that marriage is a personal commitment but still can be influenced by tradition and, in the case of a monarch, by politics and public opinion. She exhibited astonishing *self-discipline*, avoiding public criticism, media coverage, and even renouncing her royal title calmly, allowing her to uphold her values without further dispute.

The Power of Integrity

Integrity refers to a commitment to truthfulness, ensuring that actions consistently reflect one's values. It is frequently misconstrued as simple honesty. Honesty involves conveying the truth, whereas integrity represents the essence of truth in one's life. It involves honoring promises, standing against corruption, and maintaining moral values even in the face of hardship or risk. Initially, integrity may appear to be less formidable when compared with wealth, political power, or physical strength. Integrity builds trust, and trust cultivates long lasting influence. In the absence of integrity, institutions fail, relationships break down, and societies fall apart. Through the power of integrity, individuals lacking weapons or wealth can still influence the course of history.

Integrity serves as the cornerstone for communities and institutions; without it, no legal system, government, or social contract can operate effectively. On a personal level, integrity fosters resilience. An individual who embodies honesty has no reason to fear exposure or shame. Their consciousness is at peace. Even in failure, they maintain their integrity because they have not compromised their true selves. Integrity supports a clear understanding of actions taken. When principles and actions are aligned, decision-making becomes clear and uncomplicated, free from contradictions.

Integrating the Three Principles

Strength of character does not arise from a single quality but from the interaction of several guiding forces. The inner compass provides ***direction***, helping individuals remain resilient and hopeful even in difficult times. Self discipline supplies the ***structure***, ensuring that impulses and emotions are controlled so that actions remain consistent with values. Integrity is the ***binding force***, uniting direction and discipline into a coherent moral stance. When these three principles work together, they create a foundation strong enough to resist external pressures, whether in grand social struggles or in personal decisions.

The journeys of Gandhi, Malala, and Princess Mako demonstrate how these three principles (inner compass, self discipline, and integrity) are not abstract ideals but lived realities that shape both nations and individual lives.

Chapter Summary

1. Strength of character is essential for survival and growth, which is beyond wealth, strategy, or power.
2. The inner compass acts as a moral guide, helping individuals navigate hardship with honesty, courage, justice, and compassion.
3. Hard times reveal true character, stripping away illusions and showing whether values are genuine or superficial.
4. Components of the inner compass are resilience, hope, moral clarity, and self-discipline, which enable stability in adversity.

5. Integrity as the Binding Force: Integrity is the force that binds the inner compass and self-discipline together, ensuring actions are consistent with values and fostering trust and long-lasting influence.

Bibliography

1. Gandhi, M.K. *The Story of My Experiments with Truth.* Navajivan Publishing House, 1927.
2. Yousafzai, M., & Lamb, C. (2013). *I Am Malala: The Girl Who Stood Up for Education and Was Shot by the Taliban.* London: Little, Brown.
3. BBC News. (2021, October 26). *Japan's Princess Mako marries commoner Kei Komuro after years of controversy.* BBC. https://www.bbc.com/news/world-asia-59035015

Part II: Sustaining in the Long Run

4

Using Scarcity as an Opportunity

Introduction

Individuals generally consider scarcity as a problem, which means a shortage of resources, time, or opportunities that stop progress. However, history and new ideas indicate that a shortage of resources can also be become reason for creativity, perseverance, and advancement. When resources are scarce, people and businesses have to be creative. This way they are able to search for new ways to do things that they would not have considered otherwise. Scarcity may help people focus and come up with new ideas, such as when business owners look for new markets during economic downturns or when people learn new talents when they do not have much money. Instead of seeing scarcity as a problem, learning to use it as a chance may lead to development, change, and long-term success.

What are Opportunities

A beneficial circumstance or occurrence that offers an opportunity to accomplish something valuable or progress is called an opportunity. They often display themselves as chances that, if acknowledged and taken advantage can result in development, achievement in one's personal, professional, or academic life. These are like doors, and you have the power to decide whether or not to open them. Not all opportunities are created by chance; many are won with perseverance, hard effort, and inventiveness. Historical examples such as Abraham Lincoln's perseverance and the Apollo 13 mission show how scarcity can inspire human progress.

Historical case

From Hardship to Leadership: The Life of Abraham Lincoln

Abraham Lincoln served as the 16th President of the United States of America from 1861 to 1865. He was raised up in a little log cabin outside Hodgenville, Kentucky, and taught himself most of the things he knew. He eventually became a lawyer. He was a member of the Illinois legislature and the U.S. House of Representatives for only a brief period. He was elected president in a nation on the verge of collapse, and he guided the country through the Civil War, preserving the Union. As he grew up in a small wood house outside of Hodgenville, Kentucky, did not have much access to formal schooling, money, or social ties, but instead of seeing scarcity as a weakness, he used it as a strength. To understand his achievements, his account is divided into three sections: Scarcity of Resources, Scarcity of Privilege, and Scarcity of Peace. It clearly illustrates how he transformed these scarcities into opportunities for Self-Education, Relationship Building, and Leadership, which are listed below:

- **Scarcity of Resources into Opportunity for Self-Education:**
  Lincoln had merely a few books to read, but he read them numerous times and grasped them well. This scarcity of things developed his mind, enhanced his memory, and trained him in the way to learn on his own.
- **Scarcity of Privilege into Opportunity to Relationship Building:**
  He grew up in poverty, was aware of the hardships faced by the people. Because of this, he gained empathy and gained credibility by making his speeches and ideas very approachable.

- **Scarcity of Peace into Opportunity for Leadership**: As president during the Civil War, he had to deal with unity, which is one of the most valuable things a country can have. He maintained the Union and laid the groundwork for independence by using the crisis to demonstrate great leadership rather than giving in to pressure.

When Crisis Sparks Creativity: The Story of Apollo 13

Apollo 13, launched on April 11, 1970, was NASA's third crewed lunar landing. After two days of launch, an explosion of the oxygen tank occurred and disabled the spacecraft, causing astronauts James Lovell, John Swigert, and Fred Haise to struggle for their life. The three astronauts had quickly recovered from the shock and stayed calm, and NASA's quick thinking turned a tragedy into one of history's most daring space rescues. Because of the explosion which occurred earlier, power and oxygen supply in the spacecraft rapidly decreased. Mission Control in Houston swiftly prioritized astronaut safety above lunar exploration. The Lunar Module Aquarius, designed for two astronauts for two days, became a “lifeboat” for all three. In life-threatening circumstances, engineers and astronauts showed remarkable inventiveness. When the rapid increase of carbon dioxide took place, creativity played a vital role during this time. The CO_2 filters were unsuitable for the Lunar Module's system. The ground engineers created a "square peg in a round hole" solution by making use of plastic bags, cardboard, and duct tape. The crew navigated and re-entered Earth's atmosphere physically using cooperation and cleverly utilizing their resource despite bitter temperatures and limited electricity. On April 17, 1970, Apollo 13 landed in the Pacific Ocean, displaying that inventiveness and partnership could prevail over any catastrophic events that take place in life. Apollo 13 symbolizes how scarcity of resources can create opportunities for new innovations.

Persistence to Live: Sunita Williams on ISS Trip (2025)

Humanity's journey into space has always been a story of persistence, innovation, and the courage to adapt to scarcity. Among the astronauts who symbolize these values, Sunita Williams stands out as a beacon of determination and progress. Sunita Williams, an Indian Slovenian U.S. Navy officer and NASA astronaut, has spent over 322 days on the ISS in two missions (Expeditions 14/15 in 2006–2007 and 32/33 in 2012). Sunita "Suni" Williams has long been a symbol of courage, innovation, and perseverance. Her recent mission aboard the International Space Station (ISS) in 2024–2025 offers a powerful case study. Her time aboard the International Space Station (ISS) is not merely a tale of surviving in the harshness of space but a profound lesson in how persistence and innovation can transform limitations into pathways for growth.

What began on June 5, 2024, as a short-duration test mission aboard Boeing's Starliner spacecraft, was intended to last only about eight days. However, due to technical failures in thruster and helium leakage in the Starliner's propulsion system, made returning through that vehicle was unsafe. Thus, what was planned little over a week away from Earth became an **extended mission** of about 9 months. They finally returned on **March 18, 2025**, via the SpaceX Dragon (Crew-9) capsule.

Every resource is valuable on ISS. Limited resupply means managing water, food, oxygen, and power. Williams and her crew used advanced filtration systems to recycle humidity and urine water. The microgravity environment required precise meal rationing and waste management to avoid contamination. She worked hard, despite the limitations. she did experiments, spacewalks and exercise to prevent the muscle and bone loss that occurs from being in microgravity. Scarcity has effects on the individuals and spaces. Discipline, teamwork, and emotional stability were required to survive in the ISS's restricted quarters .She stated that routines, humor, and communicating with others were important ways to deal with stress. Her ability to stay positive, research, and running a space marathon shows humans adaptability under extreme conditions. Sunita Williams's story demonstrated how resource optimization, teamwork, and innovation can overcome scarcity during tough times. Her legacy inspired many astronauts and engineers who are developing sustainable systems for long-duration Moon and Mars missions.

Chapter Summary

1. **Scarcity encourages creativity and innovation**, pushing individuals and societies to find new solutions.
2. **Persistence and hard work transform challenges into opportunities** for personal and collective growth.
3. **Teamwork and adaptability** are essential to overcoming limitations and ensuring success under pressure.
4. **True progress arises from using limited resources wisely,** showing that scarcity can be a foundation for long-term development.

Bibliography

1. Goodwin, D. K. (2006). *Team of rivals: The political genius of Abraham Lincoln*. Simon and Schuster
2. Holden, H. M. (2012). *Danger in Space: Surviving the Apollo 13 Disaster*. Enslow Publishing, LLC.
3. NASA. (2025) *Sunita Williams: Astronaut Biography*. **NASA,** https://www.nasa.gov/astronauts/biographies/sunita-l-williams/biography (Accessed: 14 Oct. 2025).

5

Building Networks & Alliances

Introduction: The Web of Human Survival

Man is considered the most intelligent being in nature, even though in many aspects he lags behind other creatures. There are several traits that are more developed in other animals, such as:

- Power: Humans have less muscle power than tigers, cheetahs, elephants, or even pandas.
- Sense of direction: Sea eagles, flamingos, and pigeons excel in this area.
- Multitasking: Dogs are among the best animals in terms of multitasking abilities.
- Honesty and loyalty: Gibbons, albatrosses, and swans are known for their faithfulness, as they cannot live without their partners.

However, there are many drawbacks in human characteristics, yet strength alone is not the key to survival—it is only a part of it. The other essential factor is connection, which humans build to survive.

The previous chapters taught us that adapting to change is an art of survival, and that strength of character and values play a vital role in this process. To sustain life eventually, resource management is essential. In the same way, building networks and alliances is equally important.

Throughout history, alliances have shaped the destiny of civilizations. It found its roots from tribal communities that united for protection, to nations that forged partnerships for peace and progress. These alliances transformed humanity's journey from mere survival to flourishing societies. Even today, the ability to collaborate and form strong networks continues to define humanity's path from survival to thriving.

The Importance of People in Survival

Humans are psychological beings. They need a sense of security, and for that, they depend on society. To build a society, they must communicate with each other. This communication helps them understand the needs of others, creating a sense of belonging among individuals.

In the early days, humans faced basic survival challenges such as protecting their offspring, finding food, and seeking shelter. These needs led to the practical necessity of cooperation in human evolution. Humans discovered that mutual understanding and win-win relationships were essential for survival in a predatory world. Such mutual support fosters both resilience and innovation.

Even today, we can see how cooperation and alliances operate at the smallest level for example within a household. For instance, many Indian families follow the joint family system. This type of system not only provides a sense of security but also ensures easier access to shelter and food. It becomes easier to start a new family in a joint family setup, as elders offer emotional and financial support. Newborn babies also receive love, affection, and protection in such environments, whereas nuclear families often face more challenges when caring for newborns.

At the heart of these systems lies trust, empathy, and a shared purpose. These are the invisible threads that hold societies together. Trust allows individuals to rely on one another, reducing fear and uncertainty in daily life. It encourages openness, honesty, and collaboration. Empathy helps people understand each other's emotions and struggles, making them more willing to offer support during difficult times. It bridges personal differences and builds emotional unity. A shared purpose gives direction and meaning to these bonds, aligning personal goals with collective well-being.

Together, these values form the foundation of human coexistence. They turn temporary cooperation into lasting alliances built on respect and understanding. When trust deepens, empathy flourishes, and a shared purpose guides action, societies become more resilient, innovative, and harmonious. Such unity not only strengthens survival but also enables humanity to grow, progress, and thrive beyond mere existence.

These same principles extend far beyond families and small communities. Trust binds neighbors into communities; empathy unites diverse groups into nations; and shared purpose fuels global movements that seek justice, peace, and progress. From the formation of early tribes that depended on cooperation for survival, to modern nations built on ideals of unity and equality, and even to worldwide humanitarian movements striving for environmental protection and human rights. These forces continue to define humanity's journey. Further in chapter, The first world war, Nelson Mandela's story, and global alliances at the time of crisis exemplify the concept of unity and throws light on the importance of strong network and alliances, which helps people at the time of emergency.

Historical Perspectives: Lessons Across Time

History is recorded events, particularly people's experience, which became reference for study the nature of the event to reach some constructive outcomes.

Rebuilding After Collapse

The first world war was one of most devastating conflicts in human history. In this war, nations got destroyed, empires were knocked down. After that war generations left behind were hunted by the violence of mechanized warfare. This war had a severe impact on the life of humans. If humanity needs to survive, it needs new ways, one root not competition. To avoid such war, sustainable measures were the need of that time. This gave the platform to world's first attempt for global cooperation, which gave the opportunity to come into existence with the Nations League.

National League is established in 1920 under the Treaty of Versailles. It was the first attempt by nations to prevent war through collective efforts in areas of security, disarmament, and diplomacy. The trepidation of war was so high that survived, made the conclusion that disputes must be solved in other ways rather than bloodshed. The main core idea of nation league is trust, empathy, and shared responsibility, which are the same principle binding human societies at smaller scales.

Its early works were remarkable, as it addresses the issues of refugee resettlement, global health, drug trafficking, and labor rights. However, it had own flaws in its structural designing. Even though, the structural design was from the 28th president of the United States, Thomas Woodrow Wilson, US never joined it. Without major powers contribution its hold started loose, and its credibility suffered. The League had no real military power to enforce its resolutions, relying instead on moral persuasion and economic sanctions. Due to these, it became ineffective against aggressive regimes. After 1930 events, Japan invaded Manchuria (1931), Italy attacked Ethiopia (1935), and Germany violated the Treaty of Versailles, these flaws were much clear to the world. By the time World War II began in 1939, the League of Nations had effectively collapsed. Even though it failed in its core concept, the League left behind invaluable lessons. Its collapse taught the world that temporary alliances or symbolic cooperation are not enough to guarantee peace. Its collapse showed that to sustain collaboration, relations were needed to build mutual trust and accountability among nations.

The story of the Nations League reflects a timeless truth: survival depends not on strength alone, but on cooperation. Today, the world faces new challenges such as climate change, pandemics, economic inequality, and political conflict. the lesson remains as urgent as ever: peace and progress require more than momentary alliances. They require sustained collaboration rooted in shared purpose.

Nelson Mandela – Forging Unity After Apartheid

In early 2000's, South Africa was still healing from the deep wounds of apartheid, which a system or policy of discrimination on grounds of race. In this tough time, Nelson Mandela had stepped down as president in 1999. His leadership exemplified the principles of **building networks and alliances. Building networks and alliances refers to the process of connecting diverse individuals, organizations, and groups toward a common goal. This became mission in his post presidency period. He aimed** to unite people across divisions and mobilize collective energy for peace, development, and justice.

Even though he retired from active political participation in 1999, he emerges as grate leader for global morals. He changes his focus from politic to work for the humanity. He believed that social progress depends not on isolated efforts but on **networks of solidarity**. He started the Nelson Mandela Foundation (NMF), which became a hub for dialogue, reconciliation, and archival preservation. Through this foundation, he built partnerships between governments, NGOs, and private organizations, encouraging open discussion on issues like poverty, HIV/AIDS, and education. The NMF became a model for collaborative governance, illustrating how alliances can transform public will into sustained social change.

Mandela spoke out about AIDS in public after his son Makgatho died of it in 2005. He asked governments and societies to work together to fight the disease. Further, he established The Elders in 2007, a notable initiative for alliance-building. In order to establish an autonomous organization focused on peace, human rights, and climate justice, he gathered renowned world leaders like Kofi Annan, Jimmy Carter, and Desmond Tutu alongside Graça Machel and Richard Branson. Mandela characterized them as "autonomous global elders capable of articulating their thoughts freely and assertively."

Nelson Mandela demonstrated that leadership is not confined to holding office. it is about connecting people through purpose, compassion, and dialogue. By forging networks and alliances that transcended national, racial, and ideological boundaries, he built a framework for enduring peace and progress.

Global Alliances in the Face of Crisis

This century has had unprecedented series of global crises, such as pandemics, climate change, economic recessions, geopolitical conflicts, and technological disruptions. These challenges have transcended national borders, demanding collective responses that no single nation or organization can manage alone. The recent era has therefore witnessed a renewed emphasis on global alliances and networks. These can be built upon the principles of cooperation, shared knowledge, and mutual responsibility. From international health partnerships to climate coalitions and digital diplomacy, the modern world reflects how humanity's survival and progress depend on its ability to collaborate effectively.

The COVID-19 pandemic (2020–2022) became one of the most defining crises of the modern age. It exposed weaknesses in global systems but also demonstrated humanity's capacity for alliance building. Organizations such as the World Health Organization (WHO) coordinated worldwide data sharing, health protocols, and vaccine distribution. The COVAX initiative, led by WHO, Gavi, and CEPI, represented a crucial example of global networking. Another major arena of alliance-building in the recent era has been the global response to climate change. The Paris Agreement (2015) stands as a landmark achievement in international cooperation, where 196 countries committed to limit global warming to below 2°C.

The 21st century has witnessed the growth of strategic partnerships in the digital and economic domains with the goal of ensuring stability and innovation. Specifically in the wake of the 2008 financial crisis and the economic consequences of the pandemic, the G20 and World Economic Forum have developed into significant forums for coordinating economic recovery plans. Meanwhile, networks driven by technology, like the Digital Public Infrastructure Alliance and the Global Partnership on Artificial Intelligence (GPAI), have been developed to support data privacy, ethical technology use, and fair access to innovation. With partnerships like NATO's Cooperative Cyber Defense Centre of Excellence (CCDCOE) increasing global resilience against cyber threats, cybersecurity has also evolved into a cooperative defense area. These partnerships highlight the fact that cooperation is just as important to economic and technological security in today's globally interconnected world as competition.

Chapter Summary

1. Survival is not about strength alone but about cooperation and connection. Human progress depends on relationships built on trust, empathy, and shared goals.
2. Societal bonds start at the family level and extend to nations and the world. Emotional unity in small systems mirrors the foundation of global peace.
3. History teaches that alliances must be genuine and sustainable. The failure of the League of Nations reminds us that symbolic cooperation cannot replace accountability and trust.
4. Leadership through empathy creates lasting impact. Nelson Mandela exemplified how alliances rooted in compassion and purpose can heal divisions and inspire progress.
5. Modern crises demand collective global action. From pandemics to climate change and cybersecurity, humanity's future relies on networks that transcend borders and promote shared responsibility.

Bibliography

1. Walters, F. P. (1952) *A History of the League of Nations*. London: Oxford University Press.

2. Lodge, T. (2006) *Mandela: A Critical Life*. Oxford: Oxford University Press.
3. The Elders (2025) *About The Elders: Working for Peace, Justice and Human Rights*. Available at: https://theelders.org (Accessed: 23 October 2025)
4. World Health Organization (2021) *COVID-19 Strategic Preparedness and Response Plan*. Geneva: WHO. Available at: https://www.who.int (Accessed: 23 October 2025).
5. Gavi, the Vaccine Alliance (2021) *COVAX Explained*. Available at: https://www.gavi.org/covax-facility (Accessed: 23 October 2025).
6. G20 (2020) *G20 Leaders' Declaration: Riyadh Summit, 21–22 November 2020*. Available at: https://www.g20.org (Accessed: 23 October 2025).
7. Global Partnership on Artificial Intelligence (GPAI) (2022) *Annual Report 2022: Advancing Responsible AI*. Montreal: GPAI Secretariat. Available at: https://gpai.ai (Accessed: 23 October 2025).
8. NATO Cooperative Cyber Defense Centre of Excellence (CCDCOE) (2023) *Annual Review: Cyber Defense Cooperation in 2023*. Tallinn: NATO CCDCOE. Available at: https://ccdcoe.org (Accessed: 23 October 2025).

6

Learning from Failures

Introduction

Failure is an inevitable part of learning, yet it is indispensable for success. The survival of human life on Earth itself is the result of multiple attempts shaped by varying conditions and ultimately, through favorable ones, life found a way to thrive. Historical innovations further affirm this pattern. Bell's invention of the telephone, Edison's creation of the light bulb, and the Wright brothers' development of the aircraft, stands as remarkable examples that failure is the first step toward invention. Success is born from countless errors and repetitions. Each unsuccessful attempt compels us to explore alternative approaches and refine our understanding. Failure is not a sign of weakness; rather, it strengthens our wisdom. Building upon the previous chapter's discussion of networking and alliances, learning from both collective and individual setbacks becomes the next step toward sustainable growth. Societies and institutions that treat failure as a learning opportunity develop adaptive capacities essential for long-term development. In this context, analyzing how individuals and groups derive insight from setbacks provides a crucial perspective for achieving continuous improvement and innovation.

Why Failure is a Teacher, Not an Enemy

Repeatedly, failure seen as a mark of inadequacy rather than a step toward mastery. Society never appreciates the effort of those who failed in their context. Yet, in history, it has shown that every major achievement is rooted in unsuccessful attempts. Almost every inventor faced countless rejections, which gave impression that human progress has always depended on the courage to fail. Failure is not the opposite of success; it is the foundation upon which success is built.

In human psychology, unsuccessful attempts cultivate toughness in nature to adapt and recover in the face of adversity. Human mind has ability to rewire its expectations, develops patience, and triggers cognitive thinking capability. The deep study of the human mind confirms that brain learns more through trial and error correction rather than effortless success. Examples to prove these are countless in history. For instance, entrepreneurs like Steve Jobs, who faced rejection and removal from his own company, used failure as a springboard to reinvent innovation through Apple's revival. Another vaccine development process, developer made countless attempts before bring vaccine in status before they introduce it in public. In every case, failure acted not as an end but as a mentor guiding toward better understanding and enduring success. To understand its importance, next secession historical case studies will help.

Historical Perspectives: Lessons Across Time

Research record invention, yet history records all failure attempts before reaching its goal. As well said by Thomas Edison, "I haven't failed; I've found 10,000 ways that don't work"

The Early 1900s: Thomas Edison's Electrical bulb

In 1878, the light bulb, humanity's most significant invention, was realized after thousands failed attempts by Mr. Edison and his associates. Their first attempt was to develop carbonized compressed lampblack. Before their attempts, others had already invented various incandescent lamps, but these lamps suffered from drawbacks, such as a brief lifespan and the need for a large current to function. Their first attempts burnt out quickly, then different methods were tried, such as introducing different gases, hemp, and palmetto. Finally, bamboo was observed as the most durable filament among all. Every unsuccessful attempt made by him never deterred him but rather became data and inspiration to reach his goal with determination. He saw every mistake as a message, a clue hidden within failure, which directly points towards improvement. His laboratory became a living example of the experimental method, where success was not a single moment of triumph, but the accumulation of insights gained through repeated setbacks.

He changed his mindset to see failure as feedback rather than defeat. This changes the work environment and creates an environment favourable to innovation. Modern innovation and research are based on these failure attempts of the past, which connect curiosity with creation. Frequent failure attempts enhance understanding of the finest details of success. His attempts to develop a theory aimed not only to identify the moment of certainty for an event to occur but also to cultivate the willingness to endure uncertainty.

Edison's determination to make all failure attempts work for one eventful successful imparts a profound lesson: true failure occurs only when learning stops. Every unsuccessful experiment contributes to the collective progress of knowledge. Edison's story thus embodies a universal truth:

innovation is not about avoiding errors but about transforming them into stepping stones toward discovery.

Princess Diana: Transforming Personal Adversity into Humanitarian Impact

Princess Diana also knows for her title as "The People's Princess" and as the Princess of Wales. She was born on July 1, 1961, into the British aristocracy, where she encountered both privilege and personal difficulties, including her parents' separation. She catches the eye as public figure upon her marriage to Charles, Prince of Wales, in 1981. Their marriage is an event viewed by millions globally. The marriage, which initially regarded as a fairy-tale union, soon enough she started to encounter significant difficulties in it. Diana battled not only with the demands of royal existence, but also constant media scrutiny. All of above these, she found herself emotionally detached from her partner. These personal isolation, insecurity, and public criticism in her life intensified her feelings of failure and inadequacy within her marriage. The deterioration of communication and trust in her marital life ultimately resulted in the couple's separation in 1992. By 1996, this separation was converted into divorce. Her life illustrates the transformation of personal and public failures into purpose and social impact. Her divorce from Prince

Charles was criticized in the media, which subjected her to emotional distress and extensive criticism..

A lot of people viewed these challenges as both personal and social failures. However, she turned her challenges into opportunities based on reasoning that leads to humanitarian endeavors. As first step, she started campaigning for causes that are frequently ignored or criticized. These campaigns include AIDS awareness, leprosy treatment, and the international campaign against landmines. With her honesty regarding personal vulnerability, she challenged traditional perceptions of royalty. Her story taught us that sincerity and compassion could catalyze global transformation. She transformed emotional hardship into concrete humanitarian results. This transformation demonstrated her strength, bravery, and the capacity to learn from failures.

Princess Diana's experience is that failure is not the endpoint but a mentor guiding growth. Her life exemplified the principle that true success is measured not by the absence of failure, but by the ability to rise from it and positively impact others.

The Recent Era: Global Climate Action – Learning from Missed Targets

Over two decades, world facing its biggest challenge as climate change on the Earth. This shows urgent acknowledgement from all parts of the world and preventive measures need to be taken to stop degradation of it. Despite countless efforts of different organizations to conduct treaties, summits, and pledge to reduce, these efforts have fallen short of their goal. Uneven commitments, uneven national participation are obstacles for collective action. However, these repeated failures do not signify defeat. Instead, it becomes inspiration and valuable lessons to take effective measures to cultivate dynamic collaboration, accountability, and shared responsibility among nations.

Importantly, these failed cooperations become catalysts for innovation. Reduction of emissions of the harmful gases in environment missing the target. This accelerates research in renewable energy technologies such as solar photovoltaics, wind power, and green hydrogen. In the same way, bad policies have led to the rise of youth-led movements like Fridays for Future and Earth Uprising that demand actionable change and challenge people to stop being public complacency. As people become more aware and active, political priorities have changed. This has led governments and businesses to invest in sustainable solutions and circular economy models. In the tech world, too, past inefficiencies have led to big steps forward in areas like energy storage, carbon capture, and building infrastructure that can withstand climate change. These taught that failure over global scale can still seed the greener, wise future. What once seemed like failure now functions as feedback, pushing humanity to refine its methods, strengthen alliances, and build adaptive resilience. In this sense, the global climate movement mirrors the scientific process itself: progress through iteration, collaboration, and learning from error. The ongoing pursuit of sustainability thus stands not as a record of missed opportunities, but as a testament to the world's capacity to evolve through failure toward collective wisdom and renewal.

Chapter Summary

The chapter redefines perception of failure to see it not as a menace to success, but as a **mentor** that shapes growth, resilience, and wisdom. Failure, when embraced constructively, becomes a guide that directs individuals and societies toward continuous improvement. The take away points of chapter are:

1. **Failure is a catalyst for growth**
   It promotes reflection, adaptation, and deeper understanding.
2. **Psychological resilience grows through failure**
   Human brain learns best through correction and challenge.
3. **Modern innovation thrives on past setbacks**
   Technological progress and entrepreneurship often arise from past mistakes.
4. **Emotional Growth through Failure**
   Understanding how to process setbacks with reflection and self-compassion allows individuals to convert emotional pain into personal strength.
5. **Collective Learning and Progress:**
   When organizations and societies learn collectively from mistakes, they cultivate adaptability, innovation, and stronger systems for the future.
6. **Persistence as a Path to Sustainability:**
   Persistence converts sustainability from an aspirational goal into continuous practice; by embracing the lessons of failure, individuals and communities build habits that ensure long-term progress.

Bibliography

1. Israel, P. (1998). *Edison: A Life of Invention*. New York: John Wiley & Sons
2. Bradford, S. (2006). *Diana*. London: Penguin Books.
3. UNEP. (2023). *Emissions Gap Report 2023: Broken Record – Temperatures Hit New Highs, Yet World Fails to Cut Emissions (Again)*. Nairobi: United Nations Environment Programme.

7

Sustaining with Vision

Introduction

Almost every civilization, past or present, has faced moments of deep crisis. In such times, survival becomes the central motive of its people. Basic needs like food, water, and shelter take priority, as sustaining life becomes the immediate goal. Yet survival is only a temporary achievement. However, vision of future will become the main goal. Vision is the ability to imagine and work toward a future beyond the present struggle. The difference between these two concepts is simple but profound: survival preserves what exists, while vision rebuilds what has been lost. Civilizations that rise again after disaster are led by visionaries; those that remain trapped in fear and stagnation often fade into history. The capability of humans to envision future is most endorsing strength. Survival relies on reflex; vision relies on reflection. Societies that merely endure crises may survive for a while, but those that learn, adapt, and redirect their energy toward renewal evolve into stronger versions of themselves. When a generation develops foresight, it creates continuity between the lessons of the past with the possibilities of the future.

In early chapter, failure is explored as a teacher, which became necessary for growth. Now, journeys move beyond reaction. Having learned from failure, one must learn to see beyond it. This chapter focuses not only on recovery to sustain, but also on foresight future, the intellectual compass that guides endurance toward meaningful progress.

Looking Beyond Short-Term Survival

Survival and sustain are separated by simple line defined by the time. Survival focused immediate action; where sustains sustainability looks beyond the visible horizon. Under the pressure different short term policy and programmed was focused, However, they collapse after a period not due to lack of energy, but from lack of direction. Survival is possible with right time rection on the event, where as to sustain, right direction is needed. Ability of foresight helps to have direction to work for future. It transforms endurance from a desperate act into a deliberate process. Eminent leaders are well known for their foresight to bridge uncertainty of current period with future endorsements. They anticipated consequences. Their foresight builds structures that would outlast. They trusted their choices, though unpopular in the present. Which would prove essential to shape the future. Vision gives strength. At personal level, person, who has vision can tolerate it maximum. This means that there should be clarity in vision to struggle, which convert pain in preparation for the future endorsement. It is not always that you get results in short period of time. When success is delayed then vision sustains by motivation, which links the daily efforts to large patterns of significance. Same principle applied at national or international visions. Without long term vision, nation vision can transform into crises. Another example, airplane designs are not just Wright brother innovation for success but create legacy. Similarly, environmentalists who plant forests will never see mature act with intergenerational logic. Educators who nurture minds to think beyond examination build resilience that outlasts their careers. In each case, the present sacrifice is justified by the belief that the future will inherit the reward.

Historical Case

History provides the strongest evidence of how vision transforms endurance into achievement. To understand the importance of long vision in better ways, it is good to observe in different historical achievements how they transform vision into future endorsement. This section will give these ideas with case study of Winston Churchill, internet invention, and global sustainability movements.

Winston Churchill Vision

During the Second World War, Britain stood on the brink of collapse. Their resources were nearly depleted, collaboration from others was uncertain, and citizen morale was on the edge of falling apart. In that moment, the prime minister's leadership became more important than politics.. Winston Churchill taken the post. He had given a public address after three days taking the post on May 13, 1940. In his speech he said, "I have nothing to offer but blood, toil, tears, and sweat". This speech made the people prepare themselves for sustained endurance. He was genius to see beyond the immediate battlefield. According to his calculations victory would not bring peace, they needed plans to create peace. Therefore, he was planning post-war reconstruction and envisioning future alliances alongside efforts to defend the country. His anticipations lead to collaborating with the United States and the early framework for a united Europe. His leadership taught one lesson that endurance without vision exhausts itself.

Soldiers and citizens could bear suffering only because they trusted in the larger picture which he painted, that is, free nation. Churchill described the national goal as "victory, victory at all costs," emphasizing that without it, there would be no survival. By aligning courage with purpose, he transformed collective fear into collective faith.

The Founders of the Internet

When Churchill's vision focused on rebuilding a world, British codebreakers developed colossus set of computers. These set of computers were early versions of modern computers. Similarly, in late 20th century, people, like Vint Cerf, Tim Berners-Lee, and others, dreamed of a global network that would connect all people, long before most people had seen a computer. Their vision was not earning profit, but was connection, knowledge, and collaboration. The protocols and principles they developed became the skeleton of the modern Internet: open, collaborative, and scalable. The Internet has significantly enhanced the collective cognitive capacity of humanity, facilitating the rapid exchange of ideas across continents in mere seconds. What started as a technical investigation transformed into a social revolution. The deeper logic here is that vision is not limited to leaders or crises. Vision is also present in creation as well as intellectual courage to imagine systems that reach beyond individual lifespan or acknowledgement. The founders of the Internet understood that true innovation is an act of service to the future. True visionaries plant ideas that outlive them. Their work becomes part of the invisible infrastructure upon which others build progress.

Global Renewable Transition

Over the past three years, the globe has experienced an immense transition towards renewable energy. Rising sea levels, record heatwaves, and extreme weather events are all signs of the current, severe climate change. Now survival depends on creation and consumption of energy sources. From 2022 to 2025, countries like India, the US, and EU members stepped up their efforts to become carbon neutral and build renewable infrastructure. With record-breaking renewable capacity growth, India emerged as a global leader in large-scale solar and wind expansion. The United States' Inflation Reduction Act (2022) was another example of a policy-level proposal. Across Europe, programs like REPowerEU strengthened green energy independence, emphasizing resilience over dependence. The primary objective is not merely to endure climate stress, but to convert it into a driving force for evolution. To sustain the environment not only requires immediate action, but there should be directions to frame the future for better. Visionary policies now aim to align economic growth with ecological responsibility. The lesson is clear: modern survival depends on innovation that sustains.

Vision and Endurance

By studying historical cases of Churchill's courage, the internet pioneers' foresight, and modern change in energy sources, all shows one thread: the strength to persist guided by vision. This means that endurance and vision are interdependent. Endurance gives continuity; vision gives direction. For instance, Martin Luther King Jr.'s dream of equality lived on even after countless setbacks. Without that unwavering determination, the moral vision of justice would have turned into empty words. Europe's vision for stability after World War II required years of disciplined recovery and cooperation. Without that endurance, the vision of peace would have collapsed under fatigue and chaos. In the absence of endurance, vision exists merely as a theoretical construction that is susceptible and transient. Lacking vision, endurance transforms into mere tiredness, empty of purpose. Psychologically, vision acts as a stabilizer against despair. It transforms random suffering into purposeful effort. People who endure hardship with vision report higher resilience because they perceive meaning in struggle. Even within organizations or families, the rule is identical. A business that prioritizes innovation over short-term profit, a parent who nurtures curiosity instead of obedience, or a student who learns for understanding rather than marks. These all demonstrate the same pattern. Vision lengthens endurance by redefining purpose.

Chapter Summary

Making vision workable means turning it into structures like rules, habits, and values that guide behaviour. There are three rules that make foresight real:

1. Clarity of Purpose: Specify your objectives for sustainability. Is it freedom, innovation, equity, or the pursuit of knowledge? Vision without a definitive purpose collapse into abstraction.
2. Patience and Adaptability: Vision requires time and flexibility. Conditions vary; only adaptive vision endures.
3. Ethical foundation: A vision devoid of ethics leads to domination rather than advancement. Vision must encompass ethical considerations for both current and future generations.

To understand our action, we should reflect on the main questions such as,

1. How can I set goals that go beyond what I want right now?
2. How can my own strength help a bigger social cause?
3. How can a long-term vision change how I deal with uncertainty?

The logical path to sustainability is simple yet demanding:

- Learn from failure.
- Endure with purpose.
- Envision beyond survival.
- Build structures that preserve progress.

History honors those who not only survived but imagined what survival could mean.

Bibliography

1. Roberts, A. (2000). *Churchill: Walking with Destiny*. London: Allen Lane.
2. Abbate, J. (1999). *Inventing the Internet*. Cambridge, MA: MIT Press.
3. International Energy Agency (IEA). (2023). *World Energy Outlook 2023*. Paris: IEA.

4. European Commission. (2023). *REPowerEU Plan: Accelerating Europe's Green Transition*. Brussels: European Union Publications.

Part III: Thriving & Advanced Methodologies

8

Innovating to Stay Relevant

Reinventing Yourself and Your Methods

Reinvention is not just about changing appearance or tools but also about transforming thought processes, values, and approaches to match a changing world. Throughout history, individuals and organizations that embraced change and reimagined their methods have continued to thrive, while those bound by outdated habits gradually faded into irrelevance. In this process uncertainty plays a vital role in creating an opportunity to gain experience continuously and having courage, curiosity, adaptability, and a willingness to challenge past conventions. True reinvention emerges from the willingness to question what once brought success but is now limited and require redesigning it better for the present and future. This chapter extends the discussion of sustainability and adaptive characteristics explored earlier, focusing on how reinvention becomes a strategic tool for long-term relevance. Through an analysis of Steve Jobs' journey and his influential role in Apple's revival, it is possible to understand how resilience and creative vision can convert crisis into opportunity. His story shows what it means to reinvent yourself: not just getting back what you lost, but also changing what success means by being creative and clear about your goals.

Historical Case: Steve Jobs—Reviving Apple

Steve Jobs has a well-known personality, a most powerful, influential, visionary leader, and inspirational figure. He was co-founder member of Apple from 1976. By the mid-1980s, internal conflicts emerged between Jobs and CEO John Sculley. In 1985, the power struggle peaked. The board sided with Sculley, effectively removing Jobs from his managerial duties. Feeling sidelined and powerless, he resigned from Apple in September 1985. He went on to found NeXT Inc.; a computer company focused on advanced workstations and also purchased Pixar Animation Studios from George Lucas. Both of these moves that would later shape his return and legacy in Apple. However, he returned to Apple in the year 1997, which stands as one of history's most powerful examples of reinvention.

By the mid-1990s, Apple was losing hundreds of millions of dollars each year. In 1996, the company disclosed an account deficit exceeding $1 billion. Analysts at that time forecasted that Apple could face bankruptcy within a few months. Following Jobs' resignation in 1985, Apple launched several products; however, the majority were not popular with consumers. Apple's operating systems were becoming outdated and were unable to compete with Microsoft's Windows.

When he rejoined the company which he had co-founded, Apple was merely on the brink of collapse. He started by reshaping its philosophy by simplifying the product line, he focused on quality over quantity, and integrating functionality with design. He steps wise to achieve his main goal. His immediate focus is grouping and simplification of complex production cycle. He cut product clutter with reduction in models, even streamlining multiple models into product matrix. This step helps to speed up development cycles, which also helps to reduce the cost of the product, and clear impression on brand massage.

As second step, he priorities industrial design as strategic, by having simplicity in hardware and software with fewer buttons, cleaner UI. He takes old product return to market with new innovation such as iMac (1998). This shows pride in designing a product which enhanced product quality; engineers and designers felt their work mattered and customers also noticed these changes. Although, he also created new products like iPod, iPhone, and iPad and worked on building a strong brand identity through the "Think Different" campaign. This changed whole industries and made Apple a global model of creativity and innovation.

Furthermore, He built Apple retail stores to control customer experience end-to- end. Due to this, sales teams and retail staff became ambassadors; the company developed a unified voice. At the same time, he focused on tight supply-chain coordination and long-term supplier relationships. He also pushed for manufacturing quality and scale without losing design integrity. He institutionalized a culture within the company by encouraging other to say "no" to many ideas so that chosen ones would be exceptional. He set extremely high standards for design, and attention to detail regarding to product. Due to these steps, customers perceived Apple as uniquely premium. Beyond products, he reinvented Apple into a brand of imagination, simplicity, and human connection through technology.

Innovation as a Survival Tool

Innovation is necessary for survival in a world that is changing quickly; it is not a luxury. From adapting to rethinking new technologies and business models or personal habits, innovation keeps the momentum alive. People who see innovation as a way of thinking every day rather than a one-time event, like Jobs, stay ahead of the curve. To utilize our cognitive abilities for survival, the following is a systematic strategy to adopt innovation as a survival tool:

1. Recognize Change as Opportunity

- Accept that change is constant and inevitable.
- Instead of resisting it, let us view disruptions as chances to evolve.
- Stay curious about new technologies, trends, and social shifts.

2. Observe and Question Continuously

- Ask “Why?” and “What if?” about existing processes, products, or habits.
- Identify problems or inefficiencies that others ignore.
- Innovation starts by questioning the ordinary.

3. Simplify and Focus

- Don’t try to innovate in every direction at once.
- Pick one area where improvement creates real impact.

- Eliminating unnecessary complexity — clarity fuels creativity.

4. Combine Creativity with Purpose

- Let imagination meet practicality.
- Design ideas that solve real-world needs or enhance human experience.
- Innovation must be meaningful, not just novel.

5. Experiment, Fail Fast, Learn Faster

- Early prototypes, test ideas quickly, and learn from feedback.
- Treat failure as a step toward progress, not a dead end.
- Each failed attempt builds resilience and insight.

6. Collaborate and Share Ideas

- Innovation thrives in diverse teams where ideas collide and evolve.
- Listen to other perspectives — they often reveal blind spots.
- Build networks that support open discussion and co-creation.

7. Integrate Innovation into Daily Thinking

- Make creativity a daily habit, not a rare event.
- Encourage small, continuous improvements in work or lifestyle.
- Routine innovation keeps momentum alive and builds adaptability.

8. Lead with Vision and Inspire Others

- Clearly communicate the "why" behind your innovation.
- Motivate teams or peers to share the same sense of purpose.
- A strong vision transforms innovation from an act into a culture.

9. Reinvent Before Circumstances Force You

- Don't wait for a crisis to change.
- Regularly re-evaluate methods, products, and goals.
- Staying proactive ensures long-term relevance and growth.

10. Celebrate Progress and Reflect

- Acknowledge creative efforts and small wins.
- Reflect on what worked and what didn't.
- Gratitude and reflection sustain morale and future innovation.

Chapter Summary

This chapter highlights that survival and progress are dependent upon continuous innovation. Reinvention connects historical accomplishments with future opportunities. This study highlights the following key points:

- **Embrace Change as an Opportunity** –
  View every challenge or disruption as a chance to evolve and create something better.
- **Think Creatively with Purpose** –
  Innovation should solve real problems and improve lives, not just introduce something new.
- **Experiment and Learn Continuously** –
  Test ideas, accept failures, and use feedback to grow stronger and smarter.
- **Make Innovation a Daily Habit** –
  Integrate creativity into everyday thinking instead of waiting for special moments.
- **Lead with Vision and Inspire Others** –
  A clear purpose and shared enthusiasm turn individual ideas into lasting progress.

Bibliography

1. Gallo, C. (2010). *The presentation secrets of Steve Jobs: How to be insanely great in front of any audience.* McGraw-Hill.

9

Strategic Foresight & Risk-Taking

Introduction

All successful organizations or leaders exhibit a common trait, the ability to foresee and act before challenges escalate into crises. We call this ability strategic foresight. It is the art of predicting possible outcomes, analyzing upcoming risks, and preparing oneself up, to turn any uncertainty into opportunity. As we know, the world changes faster than ever, where all types of technology, economics, and global events evolve daily. The ability to look around the corner is necessity of today's era. It is essential for growth and survival.

Strategic foresight is not about being able to predict the future with perfect accuracy. Instead, it is about understanding pattens, interpreting signals, and preparing strategies that can adapt to change. Risk-taking or having the courage to act when the path ahead is unclear and uncertain. Every innovation or breakthrough which has happened had someone to take a calculated risk, which was based on the current knowledge of the time and preparation to face it rather than accepting blind optimism.

Predicting Challenges Before They Arrive

Calculating challenge before they appeared in problem is same as predicting weather for next day. It is similar to as sailor read the environment move with every signal it provides through clouds and winds. These signals often come in the form of shifts in behavior, innovation, policy changes, or unexpected global events. Foresight starts with observation. For instance, the development of remote work was visible years prior to the COVID-19 pandemic demanding worldwide implementation. Organizations that actively invested in digital infrastructure and adaptable work models were more well-equipped than those that responded later. Forecasting challenges requires both analytical tools and creative thinking. Tools like trend analysis, planning for scenarios, and environmental scanning assist organizations in recognizing potential futures. In addition, foresight means questioning what you think you know. Some businesses go out of market not because they are not smart, but because they think the future would be like the past. Kodak, for example, ignored early signs of digital photography's potential. In short, foresight is not fortune-telling. It is disciplined imagination, combining data, dialogue, and creativity to prepare for what comes next.

Historical Case- OpenAI's Strategic Leap with ChatGPT

In today's era, the most intensified example of strategic foresight and calculated risk is OpenAI. When OpenAI launched ChatGPT to the public in late 2022, it posed not only a challenge for the designers but also a risk of influencing global perceptions of artificial intelligence (AI). In 2025, we can see how the bold decision of OpenAI foresight the future, even their controlled risk-taking reshaped entire industries. Before this launch AI was viewed as powerful but at same time threaten humanity. Still, there was rising wave to utilize it in different tools. Slowly, people start to use AI tool comfortably, which increases demands for conversational interfaces that could understand different languages. Rather to wait for perfect AI model, OpenAI decided to act early, releasing a model that was still imperfect but powerful enough to spark imagination.

Rick is there that ChatGPT might fail in public domain, criticized for errors, bias, or misuse. Yet the company released the product open their door to end user and collect data from users at large scale. They use this collected data to improve it further. This step not only gives momentum to innovation but also towards building trust between engineers, designers and end users through timely responsiveness and openness for feedback.

Their foresight was in recognizing that public involvement was the most effective method to enhance AI responsibly. They transformed a potential risk into an advantage by giving exposure to end user of an incomplete model. In a matter of months, ChatGPT emerged as a widespread tool, utilized by students, professionals, and enterprises globally. This case highlights a fundamental principle: strategic foresight entails recognizing opportunities amidst uncertainty rather than awaiting certainty. OpenAI's success came not from avoiding risk but from understanding and managing it intelligently.

Calculated Risks Lead to Great Rewards

Taking risk is dangerous act, yet it emerges as utmost breakthrough with calculation. When decisions are made based on thoughtful analysis and preparation then possibility of success is more even with calculated risk. The stepwise process that can be used to calculate risk are:

1. **Identify the Opportunity**

   Every opportunity brings its own risk, rather asking what expect to go wrong? If we concentrate on what could be a possible gain from this opportunity? We will get purpose to work for it.

2. **Assess the Risks Objectively**

   It is always better to see and search for the potential downside of the proposed opportunity, like financial loss, reputational harm, or operational disruption. The main purpose of it is not to eliminate the proposal, rather it helps us to understand how to achieve it in best way.

3. **Gather Data and Insights**

   Institution should not be the only source instead it is better to rely on evidence collected from the data. This data is collected from historical events customer feedback, and repeated actions. Predictive analytics from this data helps transform uncertainty into measurable information. The more data you collect, the better you can anticipate outcomes.

4. **Prepare Mitigation Plans**

   Once the risk is identified, a backup plan should be developed based on its predictions. This includes identifying early warning signs, setting decision checkpoints, and defining clear escape plans. A good plan allows flexibility. Plans should have ability to shift quickly to new perspective if needed.

5. **Execute with Discipline**

   Execution needs courage, which generally get from well preparation strategy. The tracking mechanism for the process should adapt in real time. The key is to move forward confidently, not recklessly.

6. **Review and Learn**

   Following the implementation, analyze the successes and shortcomings. This phase converts experience into knowledge, ensuring that each risk, successful or not, contributes to next decisions.

Following these steps develops a culture of intelligent taking calculated risks. It educates firms that failure is not the opposite of success, but rather an integral component of the journey towards it.

The Power of Data-Backed Decision-Making

In this era, where top to bottom approaches had changed in object oriented, data is the most powerful ally of foresight and risk-taking. However, data alone is not important until it processes correctly to produce a desirable outcome. The power of data resides in its ability to uncover patterns and forecast results. Organizations which utilize data effectively are able to predict customer needs, recognize shortcomings in operations, and uncover potential risks prior to their escalation into crises.

Realistic foresight comes from the balance of quantitative analysis and human perception. Numerical data reveals occurrences, while interpretation explains what they mean. Furthermore, data-driven cultures promote transparency and accountability. When decisions are based on clear evidence, organizations can debate ideas objectively rather than emotionally. This creates a culture where innovation develops because everyone is focused on learning, not defending opinions.

Learning Mechanism

Learn, Learn, and Learn through mistakes, which is what humans always do from their birth. **Learning mechanism** turns risk-taking into growth. Learning begins with analyzing following questions:

- What did we expect?
- What actually happened?
- Why did it happen that way?
- What will we do differently next time?

These fundamental questions develop a habit of critical thinking and humility. Those who acquire the answer to these questions will get opportunities to look ahead before their competitors.

Learning mechanisms also depends on psychological safety which comes with the freedom to speak up without fear of punishment. In the end, learning turns uncertainty from a danger into an opportunity. Each challenge becomes a classroom for improvement.

Chapter Summary

Strategic foresight and risk-taking are not opposites. Rather, they are partners in progress. Foresight helps to anticipate challenges at the same time taking calculated risk helps to size the opportunities. The main points that are focused on in this chapter are:

- **Foresight Begins with Observation:** Always pay attention to weak signals such as small shifts that might hint at larger change. The earlier you notice patterns, the better you can prepare.
- **Calculated Risks Drive Innovation:** Every major breakthrough starts with courage. The goal is not to avoid risk but to understand and manage it intelligently.

- **Data is a Compass, Not a Cage:** Use data to guide decisions, but balance analytics with human judgment and creativity.
- **Learning is the True Competitive Edge:** Learn quickly from both success and failure evolve faster and more effectively.
- **Uncertainty is an Opportunity:** Instead of fearing the unknown, use foresight and data to shape it. Those who act early and adapt continuously lead the future.

Bibliography

1. Ciesla, R. (2024). *The Book of Chatbots: From ELIZA to ChatGPT*. Cham: Springer.

10

From Surviving to Sustaining in Daily Life

Introduction

Today's era, we started to race against time. Most of daily chores are to complete one task after another, meeting deadlines because tomorrow there is another task piling up. Therefore, we find ourselves on edge of survival. We focused on daily responsibilities, meeting deadlines, and managing stress, yet rarely feeling that they are progressing toward something greater. Which leads us to survive in our life. To move beyond this survival cycle and enter a state of sustainable growth, we need to create routine which is intentionally centered to support our long terms goals. Sustainability is ability to balance, focus, and adaptability between our long term goals and current state survival cycle. It can be achieved by building everyday habits that promote progress without exhaustion, achievement without burning out, and learning without losing stability. This chapter explores small, organized routines, which can help to shift our goal from merely surviving to consistently thriving. It studies the impact of daily practices, reviews actual cases from entrepreneurs, leaders, and scientists, and offers realistic insights to assist you in cultivating your own tempo for enduring personal and professional development.

The Shift from Survival to Sustainability

Survival in unfavorable environments is a natural response to pressure. Measures are focused on meeting immediate demands and staying afloat during challenging times. However, staying in these conditions for an extended period of time can cause exhaustion, inaction, and disinterest. Sustainability, on the other hand, implies establishing a pace of life that makes things continue to get better. It is not about doing more; it is about consistently doing what matters most. A healthy way of life values discipline over rapidity, thoughtfulness over action, and progress over perfection.

To make this shift, you must first recognize your current patterns. Ask yourself:

- Am I reacting to situations or proactively shaping them?
- Do my daily habits contribute to my long-term goals?
- Is my energy spent on maintaining stability or creating growth?

Getting answers to these questions can help you see the difference between where you are currently and where you desire to go. When people are aware and do something, sustainable growth starts.

Practical Routines for Sustained Growth

Practical routines form the backbone of sustainable development. They convert abstract objectives into real acts of achievement. Establishing good habits helps you avoid decision fatigue, lowers your stress levels, and makes success happen automatically.

Here are five essential routines that promote sustained growth:

- ***Planned Daily Tasks***

  Daily routines are mostly structured around clear priorities. By designing top three tasks each day, such that, ones that will help you achieve your main objectives eventually. Make intentional use of digital tools or notebooks for day planning. Making schedules for tomorrow saves hours of wasted time.

- ***Journaling and Reflection***

  Reflection enhances the ability to see ahead. Writing down your thoughts, challenges, and achievements provides clarity. This helps you to notice patterns, track progress, and adjust before small issues become major obstacles, also known as Journaling practice.

- ***Physical Health and Exercise***

  Physical activity is essential for maintaining mental and emotional stability. Regular exercise increases energy, improves concentration, and reduces stress. Even brief walks or stretching sessions can help build stability and tolerance over time.

- ***Continuous Learning***

  Sustained growth demands curiosity. Dedicated time should be scheduled for listening to podcasts or practicing new skills. Learning keeps the mind flexible and helps you stay adaptable in a changing world.

- ***Weekly Review and Adjustment***

  A weekly review transforms action into knowledge. Take dedicated time slot at the end of each week to think about what worked, what did not, and what needs to change. This practice keeps your routines flexible and your priorities strong.

When you combine all of these routines, you make a rhythm that balances work, learning, and self-care, which are all important for long-term success.

Balancing Productivity, Learning, and Self-Care

For sustainability to truly work, there needs to be balance. A great deal of people only thinks about work, thinking that being busy means making progress. But working nonstop without stopping to think or rest will eventually lead to stress. Sustainability depends on three essential variables being in balance:

- Productivity: Doing the right work efficiently.
- Learning: Expanding skills and perspective.
- Self-Care: Maintaining energy and health to continue growing.

These three things are like the legs of a tripod. If one weakens, the whole system falls apart. When professional puts work first and neglects self-care, for example, they may get things done in the short term but become exhausted in the long term. In the same way, people who only learn and never put what they have learnt into practice might not make real growth. Well-balanced routines ensure that growth remains steady, meaningful, and fulfilling. It is not enough to just get through each week; you need to build up the strength to grow over time.

Flexibility: The Secret Ingredient

Routines are important, but stiffness makes it worse to follow. Flexibility in your routine and openness to change keeps it sustainable. Life has its own wonders and event with fixed schedule; fixed routines become hard to flow with life rhythm. Unexpected events, challenges, and opportunities often disrupt even the best-laid plans. Routines which are flexible without losing their main goal are best to sustain. Routines that are sustainable change but still serve their purpose. For example, if you are unable to finish your morning exercise, opt for a brisk evening walk. If your job schedule changes, move your reflection time to the evening. The goal is to be consistent, not strict. Flexibility ensures that routines are helpful rather than restricted. Sustainability thrives when discipline and flexibility coincide.

Case Studies: Modern Entrepreneurs, Leaders, and Scientists

To see how sustainable routines work in real life, let us look at how modern achievers balance discipline and adaptability.

Elon Musk – Structured Focus and Iteration

Elon Musk holds bachelor's degrees in physics and economics at the University of Pennsylvania before briefly pursuing a Ph.D. at Stanford, which he left to start his first tech venture. His leadership positions at X (formerly Twitter), Tesla, SpaceX, Neuralink, and The Boring Company, combined with his complex management approach, innovations, and foresight for sustainable energy and interplanetary existence. Despite his demanding schedule, he follows structured routine for focused work. For optimal efficiency, he breaks his day into five-minute parts. His approach demonstrates how planning and prioritization can turn high pressure into productive outcomes. Musk also practices iterative learning, which means constantly reviewing processes and refining strategies.

Sara Blakely – Reflection and Mindful Focus

Spanx founder Sara Blakely attributes her sustained success to mindfulness and reflection. Sara Blakely pursued a degree in communications from Florida State University and thereafter worked as a door-to-door saleswoman for fax machines. She emphasizes the significance of learning lessons from failure, maintaining stability throughout swift expansion, and ensuring daily activities are driven by purpose, illustrating that emotional intelligence and self-reflection are as crucial to lasting achievement as invention and hard work. She starts her day by journaling, listing objectives and expressions of thankfulness. This strategy enables her to stay grounded while maintaining clarity during fast business growth.

Jacinda Ardern – Balance and Well-Being

Jacinda Ardern started her career as a researcher and policy advisor, encountering initial challenges in a predominantly male political environment and dealing with global crises during her leadership. Finally, she appointed as Prime Minister of New Zealand from 2017 till 2023. She demonstrated balance by setting boundaries, prioritizing rest, and promoting mental health for both her self and her team. Her leadership demonstrates that caring for well-being enhances long-term effectiveness.

Scientists and Researchers – Discipline and Experimentation

In the discipline of science, meaningful progress is achieved through systematic experimentation. Researchers follow structured research protocols such as, formulating hypotheses, conducting tests, and reviewing findings, while maintaining flexibility when outcomes contradict their expectations. The combination of structure and openness encourages creativity while ensuring robustness.

These examples show that **sustainable success is not about working endlessly but about working intentionally** with structure, curiosity, and balance.

Working Smarter, Not Harder

Practical routines are the steps that help to bridge the gap between intention towards execution. Regular practice transforms inspiration into habits and discipline into achievements. Well structured routines as invisible threads supporting your ambitions.

Working smarter means:

- Planning your day around priorities, not urgencies.
- Automating decisions where possible.
- Allocating time for learning and rest.
- Reviewing and adjusting strategies regularly.

By applying these principles, you build systems that sustain success instead of depleting it.

Chapter Summary

1. **Clarify Your Goals:** Define what *sustainability* means for you, whether it is personal growth, career progress, or emotional balance.

2. **Identify Key Habits:** Select three daily routines that directly align with and strengthen your goals.
3. **Schedule Your Energy:** Plan your most demanding tasks during peak energy periods to maximize effectiveness.
4. **Incorporate Reflection:** Review your progress regularly (means daily or weekly) to stay mindful and make meaningful adjustments.
5. **Stay Adaptable:** When routines fail or life disrupts plans, do not quit, pause, reset, and rebuild consistency.

Bibliography

1. Isaacson, W. (2023). *Elon Musk.* Simon & Schuster.
2. Blakely, S. (2021). *The Spanx story: Building success through resilience and reflection.* Random House.
3. Ardern, J. (2023). *Leadership and well-being: Reflections on empathy and balance in governance.* Auckland University Press.

The Message of the Book

The central idea of the book is about transformation. The book gradually moves from surviving life's storms to steering one's own course through them. This study demonstrate that survival is instinctive, but sustainability is intentional. The most influential figures of history did not merely stay alive; they learned, redefined, and innovated. They taught us that while purpose without endurance becomes theoretical, endurance without purpose leads to exhaustion. By integrating insights from explorers, reformers, scientists, and contemporary innovators, *From Surviving to Sustaining* connects historical context with the present. It encourages readers to think about their personal challenges, to find meaning in failure, and to cultivate a mindset characterized by foresight rather than fear. As you turn these pages, every story says that survival is not distant or historical rather it lives within each of us. Whether on the Antarctic ice, within the paths of movements for freedom, or across the digital frontiers of our era, the same truth continues:

Survival saves the moment, but vision sustains the future.

www.ingramcontent.com/pod-product-compliance
Lightning Source LLC
Chambersburg PA
CBHW050020170726
48282CB00025B/482
* 9 7 8 9 3 5 7 1 7 6 8 6 6 *